Hectic life?

Feel like you're racing along on a hamster wheel?

Want some inner peace but don't know how to achieve it?

If your answer is "yes", then be sure to read on...

What People Are Saying About
Meditation Made Simple

"Jo delivers her message with clarity and effectiveness in this easy-to-read and easy-to-do book. With step by step instructions, the reader (student) receives the full benefit of Jo's expertise as a teacher of this wonderful practice.

Having attended meditation classes given by Jo, I can say with hand on heart, that her book is a true reflection of her essence and commitment to helping others – not only as a teacher, but as a friend.

This book can help everybody on so many levels – a true gem."

Sheena Cundy
(Writer, Teacher, Spiritual Practitioner, Singer/Songwriter).

"After taking the decision to start up my own business, I sought out Jo's advice on relaxation techniques and she recommended I attend her **Meditation Made Simple** course.

Attending this course was the best thing I ever did ... I was able to try out a number of different exercises in a calm and tranquil environment and find those that best worked for me.

I would not hesitate to recommend **Meditation Made Simple** to anyone ... and particularly to those suffering from executive stress!"

Donna Williams
(Company Director, InTouchMarketing).

"As a qualified clinical hypnotherapist I was taught how difficult it is to quantify what percentage of the population are hypnotizable, because different people do not respond consistently to the same hypnotic induction.

Likewise it seems obvious that there is no "one size fits all" strategy for achieving what we call the meditative state, so the various approaches outlined here represent a brilliant introduction for anyone wishing to find out what works best for them."

John T. Sinclair Dip CAH PNLP Cert Hyp {NGH} M NCH {Lic.}
(International Rock Musician, Clinical Hypnotherapist, Motivational Coach)

"I love the simplicity of **Meditation Made Simple** - it provides a wonderful introduction for beginners to the beauty and benefits of meditation.

I also love the various suggestions of different practices which I am sure the reader will find easy to follow. I personally meditate everyday so can whole-heartedly endorse what Jo says about the benefits.

Getting into a simple practice (which Jo recommends) really can change your life. You will begin to feel much more relaxed as the stress of everyday living gradually disappears.

A little gem of a book which I highly recommend".

Sheila Steptoe
(Motivational Speaker, Coach & Author of "Master Your Own Destiny")

Meditation Made Simple

An Interactive Guide to Meditation

Jo Barnard

BALBOA.
PRESS

A DIVISION OF HAY HOUSE

ISBN: 978-1-4525-5154-8 (sc)
ISBN: 978-1-4525-5153-1 (e)

Balboa Press books may be ordered through booksellers or by contacting:

Balboa Press
A Division of Hay House
1663 Liberty Drive
Bloomington, IN 47403
www.balboapress.com
1-(877) 407-4847

Because of the dynamic nature of the Internet, any web addresses or links contained in this book may have changed since publication and may no longer be valid. The views expressed in this work are solely those of the author and do not necessarily reflect the views of the publisher, and the publisher hereby disclaims any responsibility for them.

The author of this book does not dispense medical advice or prescribe the use of any technique as a form of treatment for physical, emotional, or medical problems without the advice of a physician, either directly or indirectly. The intent of the author is only to offer information of a general nature to help you in your quest for emotional and spiritual well-being. In the event you use any of the information in this book for yourself, which is your constitutional right, the author and the publisher assume no responsibility for your actions.

Any people depicted in stock imagery provided by Thinkstock are models, and such images are being used for illustrative purposes only.
Certain stock imagery © Thinkstock.

Printed in the United States of America

Library of Congress Control Number: 2012909395

Balboa Press rev. date: 5/24/2012

Acknowledgements

Front cover painting by Rosie Hopper.
Portrait photo by Lisa at LP Photography.

***

'Meditation Made Simple' is dedicated to my Dad, Laurie Halls, who, despite his passing, still feeds me with creative inspiration, encouragement, determination and support. For this, I am eternally grateful. LYD xxx

***

Thanks so much to the supportive, loving people who surround me; demonstrating their love and kindness in many different guises. I hope you know who you are! Mum; I love you more than you will ever know. John; you are my solid rock and my best friend. Thank you for teaching me the true meaning of unconditional love. Heartfelt thanks to my beautiful sons, Lewis and Max, who teach me far more than I will ever teach them. And finally, thanks to those who I have yet to meet, learn from, and be inspired by.
Isn't life exciting! xxx

***

"He who lives in harmony with himself, lives in harmony with the world."

Marcus Aurelius

CONTENTS

PART THREE -

Foreword

by Chrissie Astell

What a delight to be asked to write the foreword for Meditation Made Simple.

There has been a steady rise in interest in self-help books, spiritual workshops, complimentary medicine and holistic lifestyle events over the past twenty years and yet although many of us have enough of these books to start a lending library, some can seem complicated.

And how many of us put even the most inspired lifestyle teachings into daily practice?

Yet with all the stresses and pressures placed upon us (which seem to me to be increasing) in our everyday lives, even the idea of learning a 'new' skill, or somehow fitting it in to our already frantic routines, can seem daunting.

One of the most ancient and widely taught key tools to well-being and life improvement is daily meditation.

Science has confirmed that meditation lowers blood pressure, reduces stress (emotional, physical and mental) and assists in healthy body functions of respiration and elimination. Meditation is calming to the senses, helps us to get a better sleep, increases concentration and memory, enables easier relationships, and can increase libido! Now who amongst us cannot find at least one aspect from the list we would like to improve?

I hear so many of my own students expressing the knowledge that regular meditation practice would help, but they just don't have the know-how or time to fit it into a daily routine.

As we become calmer, happier individuals, we create an inner peace which then radiates out into our relationships, our home and our environment. We can create a peaceful inner world and a better world to live in.

Jo's passion for helping others to achieve this inner peace and indeed her desire for a better world for her own children and everyone else's, has spurred her into sharing her techniques with us in a beautifully grounded and simple approach to meditation.

Delightfully easy to read, and designed with space to record your feelings and experiences as you practise, you can learn to meditate in your own space, and in your own time.

If you are seeking a calmer, more peaceful, healthier and relaxed life… then what better place to start than right here, with Meditation Made Simple.

Inner peace leads to world peace, and it all begins with you!

My love and blessings,
Peace be with you.

Chrissie xx

Chrissie Astell
Best Selling Spiritual Author, Teacher & Facilitator
Trustee & Minister with Essene Network International
www.AngelLight.co.uk

PREFACE

Ok, let's face it; life doesn't always look like a bed of roses...

Sometimes it can be wonderful; full of joy and sheer delight. Everything seems to flow in the right direction. Magical moments touch our hearts, make us smile, laugh, sing, or feel full of love and happiness. We feel connected to everything and everyone that surrounds us, and we are harmonious and positive in our existence.

And at other times, life can appear to be quite the opposite; sad, unfair, frustrating, overwhelming, exhausting; an uphill battle. You get my drift – I know you do!

As we travel along life's path, we each have our own obstacles, our own hurdles to contend with and overcome. And these difficulties can trigger all sorts of emotions which, in turn, can create blockages to our happiness if we allow them to magnify.

The more we focus on these negative incidences, the more obstructive and insurmountable these blockages become. We are unknowingly giving our power over to negative emotions...feeding them. And the sad thing is, the beauty and wonder that surrounds us every day is no longer even noticed, let alone experienced.

The power of the mind is immense; and it certainly likes to be busy! But amazing as the mind is, it doesn't always act in our best interest. We need it for sure, but we also need to learn to put it down for a while - to breathe, to be still, to be at peace with the world, and to see that, despite these obstacles, *life is good!*

When we are in this peaceful space, we begin to view these obstacles more objectively with detachment. We no longer feel so caught up in the negative emotions that we have unconsciously associated with these challenges. Suddenly, we are merely an observer – an outsider looking in. And oh how clear the situation looks, now that we are free from it!

So, together, let us begin to explore a handful of simple techniques, and discover how you too can free your mind through meditation, creating the space to simply be the beautiful soul that you were born to be...

INTRODUCTION:

This book brings with it a simple message; that **anyone (including you!) can learn to meditate**, regardless of culture or belief system. It's simply a matter of finding a method that works for you as an individual.

Together, we will explore various basic techniques to discover which ones resonate most with you. Building your chosen technique/s into your everyday life can and will reap massive rewards on so many levels.

To get the most from this book, I recommend that you work through it in the suggested order at your own pace. There are plenty of spaces to record your own personal findings throughout, making this not just a book, but a truly personal and interactive experience.

I hope you enjoy this journey of self-discovery, and benefit from it as much as I have.

With love,

Jo Barnard
www.you-time.com

Meditation

Made

Simple

PART ONE

Useful Information

What Meditation Is...

Meditation is the process of turning our attention away from the busy, wandering mind (thus releasing ourselves from negative thought patterns and emotions) in order to be who we truly are in the present moment. This can be achieved by focusing our minds either on something specific, or by consciously following our train of thoughts objectively.

To lose ourselves in something creative like painting, sewing or writing is an effective form of meditation as it switches off the chattering mind and focuses us on one thing only – the job in hand.

And for those of you who enjoy gardening, perhaps you'll agree that weeding the garden, whilst a seemingly mundane task, can be highly therapeutic for the soul. A bit of mind-numbing can really help!

Often we enter a meditative state without even realising; gazing dreamily out of a window perhaps, or going into a daze. By doing this, we are unconsciously giving our thinking mind a much needed break.

The goal of meditation is to train your mind to work in your best interest; as a great ally, rather than a destructive force.

"To lose ourselves in something creative is an effective form of meditation."

Training the mind to think peaceful thoughts...

We may find that reading a book, or watching tv before we go to sleep at night, helps to shut off the thinking mind.

Although these methods can serve a purpose to an extent, their content, if not peaceful, can also have a detrimental effect if unpleasant emotions are stirred. This may result in disturbed, stressful sleep, and therefore, in us waking up feeling more tired than when we went to bed!

It is therefore so important to be conscious of what type of information or stories we are feeding our minds with, and when. If we want a peaceful night's sleep, we must encourage our minds to think peaceful thoughts.

Rarely do I choose to watch the news before I go to bed these days, as the stories covered are often pretty harrowing.

Although I like to keep up to date with what's going on in the world, I prefer to catch the morning summary instead, and read something positive or loving before I go to sleep at night.

"If we want a peaceful night's sleep, we must encourage our minds to think peaceful thoughts."

...And What Meditation Is Not...

To dispel a few myths...

Meditation itself is not solely connected to Eastern religions (although it is practised more widely in the East than in the West). Regardless of religion, culture or personal beliefs, meditation can be practiced by anyone.

Meditation is not necessarily about being holy or connecting to the Divine. You needn't be religious in order to practise – we can all gain from the vast array of benefits.

You do not need to be able to sit in the lotus position in order to meditate effectively. No special sitting postures are necessary. Sitting on a cushion or chair with your back straight, or lying down, is perfectly adequate.

"Regardless of religion, culture or personal beliefs, meditation can be practised by anyone."

Why Meditate?

There are so many beneficial reasons to bring meditation into our lives. The examples below are ones that I have experienced, either personally, or through my work as a therapist and teacher, and so I feel confident to share them with you. I'm sure there are numerous other benefits too – ones which I look forward to discovering and sharing with you at a later date!

"Some meditations can help you transform negative emotions into positive ones."

- Meditation has the potential to help you create a better life for yourself.

- It can increase energy levels and also your enjoyment for life.

- Simply meditating on your breath can lower your blood pressure, slow down your heart rate, and decrease anxiety levels.

- Regular meditation can help with pain management, it can heal illness, and it can prevent illness from occurring.

- Meditation sharpens your mind and brings about greater powers of concentration and focus.

"Meditation can help you to understand your soul's purpose."

- Meditation can help you to balance your emotions. Some meditations can help you transform negative emotions into positive ones. This is very powerful.

- If you feel caught up in materialist matters, meditation can help you to understand the true meaning of your destiny – why you are here - your soul's purpose.

- Meditation provides you with an opportunity to check in with yourself, and make sure you're on track with where you want to be going.

- It encourages your natural intuitive wisdom to come forth and become clear.

- From this useful insight, you can draw your own answers to your problems and dilemmas, without the need to seek the opinions of others (which may not necessarily be right for you).

Why Free Your Mind?

Of course we need our minds in order to carry out tasks and get jobs done, but we need to understand that the mind is simply a tool that can be picked up and used when needed, and then put down again. Putting it down allows us to be who we truly are, in the present moment. And realising this can be very powerful indeed.

Carrying too much in our minds, and not switching our thoughts off, can lead to high stress levels, which often results in ill health and/or insomnia. Stress is usually caused by us allowing our negative emotions, such as anxiety or anger, to take over us and become all-encompassing.

A useful point to keep in mind, is that those negative thoughts and feelings are related to either past events, or future worries. None of those things are happening now – the past is gone and tomorrow never comes. The only thing that is ever real is the present moment – the now. To meditate is to be in the present. And when we are totally in the present, we can experience an amazing sense of peace and liberation.

Eckhart Tolle's wonderful book, 'The Power of Now', talks about this point at length. It is truly inspirational and well worth reading.

*"An important thing to realise and remember is that **you are not your mind** and **your mind is not you.**"*

How Will Meditation Affect Me?

To begin with, you may feel frustrated, as the process will probably feel un-natural to you, and possibly somewhat of a chore. It is very easy to give up, thinking that you can't do it and that you've failed.

"Am I doing it right?", *"This is really boring"*, *"I haven't got time for this"*, are all thoughts that I struggled with at the beginning (and occasionally still do now!).

But the realisation that such thoughts come from giving too much power to the mind, gives us all the more reason to persevere and learn to train it effectively! And it does get easier - I promise. In fact, once you've experienced the incredible benefits, you won't want to stop!

It's important to note that various things can surface during a meditation, and we can choose to either look at those things head-on, or bury them back down to deal with at a later date. For this reason, it is possible to feel quite emotional during a meditation.

Please don't be alarmed or let this deter you from your practise. It's all good stuff!! Generally, a meditation session is a very peaceful, balancing and enjoyable experience.

"To begin with, the process will feel unnatural to you. Please don't let this deter you from your practise. "

Anyone Can Meditate

Many people who try meditation find it difficult, and quickly conclude that it's not for them.

"I can't meditate, it's just too difficult"
"I can't get these thoughts out of my head"
"I can't sit still for long enough"

These are comments that I've heard so many times along the way, but please don't give up.

Rest assured that **you can and will learn to meditate if you want to** – we just need to find a way that works for you. Your intention and commitment to practise, teamed with an effective method for you, is a concrete recipe for success.

Some people, for example, are very visual, and tend to respond well to guided meditations, like the ones on the you-time website. Other people, however, may prefer a different technique – something more structured perhaps.

We will shortly begin to explore a handful of basic meditation techniques to find which works best for you. But before we begin, I'd like to share a few useful tips with you to help make the process a little easier…

"Anyone can learn to meditate – it's simply a matter of finding a method that works for the individual."

Top Tips To Get You Started...

- Meditate regularly – daily if possible. Find a time of day that suits you and stick to the same time every day so that it becomes a habit. Don't beat yourself up if you find this difficult. If you miss a day, forgive yourself and make the intention to go back to it tomorrow. There's no set deadline here.

- The numerous benefits of meditation will accumulate gradually, so please be patient. Don't forget that "Rome wasn't built in a day"! Little and often is better than not at all. Be gentle with yourself.

- It's easier to meditate on an empty stomach, as foods stimulate the mind and make the process more difficult. First thing in the morning and last thing at night may work well for you for this reason.

"Always breathe from the abdomen rather than the chest."

- Create a nice, peaceful space to carry out your practice and ensure you won't be disturbed. You may wish to light candles, burn oils or incense, and have a shawl or blanket especially for your meditation.

- Wear loose, comfortable clothing and make sure your feet are warm and cosy.

- Have a good stretch before you start. This will help to relax the body.

- Set the intention to receive whatever it is that you currently need from this meditation session.

- Keep your mind and your heart open to whatever arises during your meditation.

- Always breathe from the abdomen (stomach area) rather than the chest. This depth of breath in itself is very healing.

- At the end of each meditation, spend a few moments appreciating the experience.

PART TWO

Let's Get Started

Simple Meditation Techniques To Try Alone

Guided meditations are wonderful, as they allow someone else to take you to a different place in your mind.

It is, however, perfectly possible to find that space without assistance from anyone other than yourself. In fact, many people prefer to meditate alone.

There are so many different techniques to try, and it is important to discover which ones best suit you.

Some people, for example, prefer to meditate with their eyes closed, while others like to focus on something with their eyes open.

In the pages that follow, you will find a handful of basic techniques to get you started. Once you have found your preferred method/s, you can add in new elements to mix things up a little. The list of possibilities with meditation is endless…

As we go along, it is useful to make notes of your findings. What did you experience? How did you feel? Did you like this method?

"In this part of the book, you will find a few basic techniques to try."

To enhance the experience further, you could play some gentle music softly in the background.

For each of these exercises, I suggest setting aside at least 30 minutes to carry out the meditation, appreciate the experience, and document your findings in the pages that follow.

Please remember to work at your own pace. There's no time limit, and it's important to experience each technique fully before moving on to the next one.

Meditation 1

Counting The Breath

"This simple but highly effective technique can be practised easily whenever tension arises."

Sit comfortably with your back straight. Relax your shoulders so that they are level, and rest your hands gently on your knees.

Lower your eyes and focus about a metre in front of you, or close your eyes if you prefer.

Breathe normally through your nose, allowing your abdomen rather than your chest to rise and fall with every breath.

Relax any part of you that is tense.

Begin counting your breath on each exhalation, and when you reach ten, begin again, counting from one to ten on the out-breath, and so on.

Whenever a thought intervenes, simply acknowledge it, let it go, and return to counting your breath.

After ten minutes or so, end your session and spend a few moments appreciating your experience.

Top Tip –

If you like this method, you can use it anywhere at any time.

If you go for a walk or a run, try counting each step. This enhances your connection with the solid earth beneath you, helping you to feel grounded. Great if you're feeling stressed, emotional or overwhelmed.

*So...how did you find **counting the breath**?*

Use these pages to record your findings...

Date of meditation:

How I felt before the meditation:

How I felt during the meditation:

How I felt after the meditation:

Date of meditation:

How I felt before the meditation:

How I felt during the meditation:

How I felt after the meditation:

Date of meditation:

*How I felt before the
meditation:*

*How I felt during the
meditation:*

*How I felt after the
meditation:*

Date of meditation:

*How I felt before the
meditation:*

*How I felt during the
meditation:*

*How I felt after the
meditation:*

Notes:

Meditation 2
Flickering Flame

You will need to light a candle for this one (unless you happen to have an open fire on the go!).

Dim the lights and sit a few feet from your candle, ensuring a clear view of the flame.

Keep your eyes focused on the candle flame throughout the meditation.

As you breathe in, imagine its pure white healing light filling your body.

As you breathe out, imagine that any negative thoughts or feelings are leaving you in the form of black smoke.

After ten minutes or so, end your session and spend a few moments appreciating your experience.

Please note that your eyes may take a few minutes to re-adjust again.

"This is a lovely meditation to practice on dark evenings. Why not combine it with a relaxing soak in the bath?"

Top Tip –

If this method works for you, you can choose to focus on other moving objects too, such as:-

- the flames from an open fire
- fish swimming around in a fish tank
- trees or long grass swaying in the breeze
- the tide coming in an out

The list really is endless. Just find something that works well for you.

*So...how did you find **the flickering flame**?*

Use these pages to record your findings...

Date of meditation:

How I felt before the meditation:

How I felt during the meditation:

How I felt after the meditation:

Date of meditation:

How I felt before the meditation:

How I felt during the meditation:

How I felt after the meditation:

Date of meditation:

How I felt before the meditation:

How I felt during the meditation:

How I felt after the meditation:

Date of meditation:

How I felt before the meditation:

How I felt during the meditation:

How I felt after the meditation:

Notes:

Meditation 3

Transform Negative Emotions Into Positive Ones

"If we give our minds too much power, our negative emotions can be all encompassing."

Sit comfortably with your back straight, resting your hands comfortably in your lap.

Think of a negative feeling you'd like to transform e.g. anger, fear, resentment etc.

Then think of something positive you'd like to replace it with e.g. love, trust, or understanding. In other words, the opposite emotion.

Take a few deep breaths, breathing from the abdomen rather than the chest.

As you exhale, breathe out your negative emotion, blowing it away.

As you inhale, breathe the positive emotion right into your core, and allow it to stay.

Continue this process until your negativity lessens.

Sit quietly and enjoy focusing on the positive feelings for five minutes or so.

Spend a few moments giving thanks for what you have experienced.

Top Tip –

Remember that our life is what our thoughts make it, so transforming your negative thoughts and feelings into positive ones will help you to move forward in an optimistic, constructive and loving way.

To take this exercise one step further; as your negative feelings lessen, begin to focus purely on the positive emotion; breathing it in, and then blowing it out to all other living beings.

So...how did you find negative into positive?

Use these pages to record your findings...

Date of meditation:

How I felt before the meditation:

How I felt during the meditation:

How I felt after the meditation:

Date of meditation:

How I felt before the meditation:

How I felt during the meditation:

How I felt after the meditation:

Date of meditation:

How I felt before the meditation:

How I felt during the meditation:

How I felt after the meditation:

Date of meditation:

How I felt before the meditation:

How I felt during the meditation:

How I felt after the meditation:

Notes:

"...the best thing one can do when it is raining is let it rain."

Henry Wadsworth Longfellow

"All you need is love."

The Beatles

Meditation 4

Meditating On A Word Or Phrase

Find a word or phrase that resonates with you. It could be taken from a song or poem perhaps, or from a conversation you've heard or shared maybe. If you like to work with spiritual cards for example, then you could draw a card and meditate on its message. Or maybe you've been inspired by a positive affirmation or quotation.

Sit comfortably and quietly, with your word or phrase either in your mind, or in front of you.

Breathe slowly, and welcome in the meaning and the message of your chosen word/s. Allow the true meaning to touch your heart. Feel it fully.

Acknowledge any thoughts, feelings or images that may emerge.

Continue with your contemplation for ten minutes, giving thanks for any messages or enlightenment that you have received during the process.

Top Tip –

Words are all around us every day. Meditating on a simple word or phrase can be incredibly powerful.

When you listen to music, pay close attention to what is being said. Open your eyes, ears and heart to words.

*How did you find **meditating on a word/phrase?***

Use these pages to record your findings…

Date of meditation:

How I felt before the meditation:

How I felt during the meditation:

How I felt after the meditation:

Date of meditation:

How I felt before the meditation:

How I felt during the meditation:

How I felt after the meditation:

Date of meditation:

*How I felt before the
meditation:*

*How I felt during the
meditation:*

*How I felt after the
meditation:*

Date of meditation:

*How I felt before the
meditation:*

*How I felt during the
meditation:*

*How I felt after the
meditation:*

Notes:

Meditation 5

Meditating On An Image Or View

"Open your mind and heart to your chosen view, allowing it to speak to you."

Choose an image that you feel drawn to. It could be a painting or drawing, an image on a poster, a photo perhaps, an object, a view, or even a symbol or shape.

You may really love this image, or you may find it unattractive. Whatever it may be, make sure you find it interesting on some level.

Sit comfortably with your chosen image in front of you, preferably placed at eye level.

Relax your body and allow your breathing to become deeper and slower.

Focus your attention on your chosen view, relaxing and softening your gaze, and allowing your eyes to be drawn further and further into the image. What does this image tell you? What do you see?

After five minutes or so, bring your attention back to the room, and give thanks for your meditation.

Top Tip –

Softening your gaze allows you to see the aura that surrounds your chosen image. With practise, notice if any colours or lights emerge.

How did you find **meditating on an image/view?**

Use these pages to record your findings…

Date of meditation:

How I felt before the meditation:

How I felt during the meditation:

How I felt after the meditation:

Date of meditation:

How I felt before the meditation:

How I felt during the meditation:

How I felt after the meditation:

Date of meditation:

*How I felt before the
meditation:*

*How I felt during the
meditation:*

*How I felt after the
meditation:*

Date of meditation:

*How I felt before the
meditation:*

*How I felt during the
meditation:*

*How I felt after the
meditation:*

Notes:

Meditation 6

Mindful Eating

To be mindful of something is to be intensely aware of it. In other words, our mind is completely focused on the one thing in hand (like our breathing and counting exercise earlier).

To eat mindfully, is to totally connect with our food, without the interference of other mental distractions.

So many of us rush our food in order to move onto the next thing, but how many of us truly savour every mouthful and feel thankful for the joy that food can bring?

Next time you sit down to eat, pay close attention to the whole experience by giving total focus to every mouthful. How many times do you chew your food before you swallow? Whereabouts in your mouth can you taste the different flavours? Which teeth are you using to do most of the chewing?

"To eat mindfully is to form a loving relationship with our food."

Try to block out all other distractions and concentrate on the real pleasure that food can bring.

When you have finished, spend a moment being thankful for what you have eaten.

Top Tip –

When we relax our body and mind, our food not only tastes better, but it has the chance to digest properly, reducing the occurrence of indigestion, heartburn, IBS and wind. We also become more aware of when our stomach is actually full, preventing us from over-indulging.

*So…how did you find **mindful eating?***

Use these pages to record your findings…

Date of meditation:

How I felt before the meditation:

How I felt during the meditation:

How I felt after the meditation:

Date of meditation:

How I felt before the meditation:

How I felt during the meditation:

How I felt after the meditation:

Date of meditation:

How I felt before the meditation:

How I felt during the meditation:

How I felt after the meditation:

Date of meditation:

How I felt before the meditation:

How I felt during the meditation:

How I felt after the meditation:

Notes:

45

Guided Meditations

"*All you need to do is allow yourself enough time to benefit fully from the process.*"

Guided meditations involve listening to an audio track which gently guides you through a meditative process.

There are so many options available; some for relaxation, some for re-energising, some for problem solving - the list is endless! Some tracks will transport you to a place of peace and beauty where you can escape to for a little while. All you need to do is allow yourself enough time to benefit from the process – the length of the track, plus five minutes or so to come round again at the end.

Guided meditations work well for many people, but again, they are not for everyone. I have found that the majority enjoy and benefit from them, but some people may have trouble visualising certain scenarios.

It is also important to add here that not all voices, tones and accents will resonate with you.

If, for example, the speaker's pace is too fast or abrupt for your liking, you may wish to try a few different ones before writing off guided meditations altogether.

For the purpose of this exercise, I have included access to a free meditation for you, guided by myself, called 'Relaxing The Body'.

Again, set aside approximately 30 minutes, log on to the following web page, experience the meditation and record your findings.

http://www.you-time.com/Meditation.html

If you have any problems accessing the meditation, please email me : jo@you-time.com

If you enjoy it, there are many more to try. Check out the shop page on my website to see what's available :

http://www.you-time.com/Shop.html

*So...how do you find **guided meditations?***

Use these pages to record your findings...

*Name of
meditation:*

Meditation by:

*Date of
meditation:*

*Length of
meditation:*

*How I felt before
the meditation:*

*How I felt during
the meditation:*

*How I felt after
the meditation:*

*Name of
meditation:*

Meditation by:

*Date of
meditation:*

*Length of
meditation:*

*How I felt before
the meditation:*

*How I felt during
the meditation:*

*How I felt after
the meditation:*

Notes:

*Name of
meditation:*

Meditation by:

*Date of
meditation:*

*Length of
meditation:*

*How I felt before
the meditation:*

*How I felt during
the meditation:*

*How I felt after
the meditation:*

Notes:

*Name of
meditation:*

Meditation by:

*Date of
meditation:*

*Length of
meditation:*

*How I felt before
the meditation:*

*How I felt during
the meditation:*

*How I felt after
the meditation:*

Notes:

PART THREE

Continuing Your Practise

I hope you have enjoyed exploring these meditation techniques.

By now, you will probably know which methods work best for you and you can begin to build them into your everyday life.

To get the most from meditation, it is best to carry out your practise every day. To make this achievable, it's a good idea to make it a habit. Once that habit is formed, it becomes almost second nature.

On the understanding that habits take 21 days to form, I would advise that you begin by dedicating at least fifteen minutes, preferably at the same time every day, for three weeks, to your practise.

If ever you get disheartened, please remember that a combination of the "3 Ps" will always lead to your success with meditation.

These are;

1. **Practise.** In other words, do it; get on with it; make time to meditate.

2. **Patience.** Instead of wishing we were masters of our practise, we need to have faith that we will develop at a pace that's right for us. Let's look back and see how far we've come already.

3. Persistence. This is our commitment to keep going and not giving up.

We need all of these Ps in equal measures.

Without patience or persistence, we simply would not be able to practise.

Recording Your Findings

Keeping a personal record of your meditative experiences allows you, not only to track your progress, but also to understand yourself better.

It's always interesting to look back on past experiences and see how things have changed for you. You'll be reminded of just how far you've come! It is for this reason that I've included a Meditation Record for you in the pages that follow.

"Watch your own personal patterns and cycles emerge."

Keeping a personal diary is also an excellent thing to do. Just a few lines each night before you go to bed can be so enlightening to look back on, as your own personal patterns and cycles begin to emerge in black and white!

How you've felt physically and emotionally, how well you've slept, what you've eaten, what your energy levels are like etc, are easy to record, and really do teach you so much about yourself.

I recommend that you also try listening to a variety of other guided meditations which can really help with relaxing and/or re-energising.

"try listening

to a variety

of other

guided

meditations"

If you enjoyed the Relaxing The Body track featured earlier, you can find a whole series of downloadable guided meditations at

<u>www.you-time.com</u>

These include Clearing The Mind, Problem Solving, Letting Go, Awakening The Senses, A Journey Through Your Chakras, plus many more.

You can also check out some other great websites which I've suggested in the Recommended Resources section at the back of this book.

And finally, may I take this opportunity to wish you an abundance of peace, positivity and pure joy, as you continue with your onward journey of enlightenment and personal growth through meditation.

You can do it! I know you can! xxx

Your Meditation Record

My Meditation
Record

Date:

Which meditation:

My experience:

Date:

Which meditation:

My experience:

Date:

Which meditation:

My experience:

Date:

Which meditation:

My experience:

Date:

Which meditation:

My experience:

My Meditation Record

Date:

Which meditation:

My experience:

Date:

Which meditation:

My experience:

Date:

Which meditation:

My experience:

Date:

Which meditation:

My experience:

Date:

Which meditation:

My experience:

My Meditation
Record

Date:

Which meditation:

My experience:

Date:

Which meditation:

My experience:

Date:

Which meditation:

My experience:

Date:

Which meditation:

My experience:

Date:

Which meditation:

My experience:

My Meditation Record

Date:

Which meditation:

My experience:

Date:

Which meditation:

My experience:

Date:

Which meditation:

My experience:

Date:

Which meditation:

My experience:

Date:

Which meditation:

My experience:

About The Author

Jo Barnard is married with two sons, and runs a holistic well-being practise, "you-time", in Essex, England, offering various therapies, workshops, and Reiki courses. She also runs a monthly meditation group and a Reiki share group.

Jo's students have been the inspiration behind her focus on making meditation simple, accessible and enjoyable for all.

Her guided scripts are available in audio format for those who wish to be led through different meditative scenarios.

Jo organises weekend retreats for those who wish to escape the daily grind to relax and discover more about themselves through meditation and spiritual practice.

She also organises holistic events for companies who wish to treat their VIP clients to some time out or a well-deserved pamper.

For more information, please visit **http://www.you-time.com**, or email **jo@you-time.com** .

You can also connect with Jo via Twitter @jo_barnard, or on Facebook or Linkedin.

Other Material by Jo Barnard

Jo is continually writing and producing new tools and resources that will empower you to help yourself. These products come in various formats:– e-Books, audio downloads, videos, tool kits and more.

Should you wish to take it a step further, there are also some lovely guided meditation scripts available that you can read aloud to others.

Jo also offers "The Complete Meditation Experience" – a wonderful kit that helps you to set the scene for meditation and explore different ways to practise.

How To Order These Products:

Jo's products are available to purchase online through her website:
http://www.you-time.com

Should you prefer to make payment by post, you can also find out how to do this on the website. Simply visit the 'Shop' page.

Jo's Other Offerings:

(current at time of print)

Courses:

Jo uses traditional Eastern teaching methods in her Reiki courses (Usui Reiki Ryoho).

- Reiki Level 1, 'Shoden'
- Reiki Level 2, 'Okuden'
- Reiki Level 3, 'Shinpiden'

Workshops:

- 'Meditation Made Simple'
- 'Aromatherapy for Home Use'
- 'Crystal Healing for Home Use'
- 'Re-balance Your Life'
- 'Discover Your Own Way Forward'

Treatments:

- Reiki
- Aromatic Massage
- Indian Head Massage
- Holistic Facials
- Spiritual Card Readings

"The Complete Meditation Experience"

by Jo Barnard

This kit includes:

Aromatherapy oil burner
2 x aromatherapy oils
Aromatherapy guided meditation CD
Crystal Meditation Kit*
*7 x chakra cards & 7 x crystals
Crystal guided meditation CD
2 x quality boxes incense
Incense ash-catcher
Glass votive and tealight
CD collection of guided meditations
(inc. music-only tracks)

While stocks last

Please visit **www.you-time.com** for more details and to order your **complete meditation experience.**

Recommended Resources

Websites:

www.you-time.com
www.freemeditation.com
www.the-guided-meditation-site.com
www.soundstrue.com
www.whatmeditationreallyis.com

Books:

The Power of Now, by Eckharte Tolle
Peace Is Every Step, by Thich Naht Hanh
The Language of Letting Go, by Melody Beatty

Suggested tools to enhance your meditation:

- **Relaxing music**
- **Aromatherapy oils**
- **Crystals**
- **Divination/oracle/meditation cards**
- **Guided scripts (to read aloud with others)**
- **A meditation timer**

Please note, Jo offers aromatherapy meditation kits, crystal meditation kits, guided scripts, and "The Complete Meditation Experience".
*Please visit **www.you-time.com** for details.*